P4

The Amish

Consulting Editors

The Amish

Fred L. Israel

Sandra Stotsky, General Editor
Harvard University Graduate School of Education

CHELSEA HOUSE PUBLISHERS

New York • Philadelphia

CHELSEA HOUSE PUBLISHERS

Editorial Director: Richard Rennert
Executive Managing Editor: Karyn Gullen Browne
Copy Chief: Robin James
Picture Editor: Adrian G. Allen
Creative Director: Robert Mitchell
Art Director: Joan Ferrigno
Production Manager: Sallye Scott

THE IMMIGRANT EXPERIENCE

Editors: Annie McDonnell and Reed Ueda

Staff for THE AMISH

Copy Editor: Apple Kover
Assistant Designer: Stephen Schildbach
Cover Illustrator: Jane Sterrett

First Printing

1 3 5 7 9 8 6 4 2

Library of Congress Cataloging-in-Publication Data

Israel, Fred L.
   The Amish / Fred L. Israel.
      p. cm.—(The immigrant experience)
   Includes bibliographical references and index.
   Summary: Surveys the history, beliefs, and customs of the Amish.
   ISBN 0-7910-3368-6.
      0-7910-3390-2 (pbk.)
   1. Amish—United States—Juvenile literature. [1. Amish.] I. Title.
II. Series.
BX8129.A6I77   1996   95-34008
305.6'87—dc20   CIP
                                                   AC

CONTENTS

THE IMMIGRANT EXPERIENCE

CHELSEA HOUSE PUBLISHERS

A
NATION OF
NATIONS

DANIEL PATRICK MOYNIHAN

The Constitution of the United States begins: "We the People of the United States. . ." Yet, as we know, the United States was not then and is not now made up of a single group of people. It is made up of many peoples. Immigrants and bondsmen from Europe, Asia, Africa, and Central and South America came here or were brought here, and still they come. They forged one nation and made it their own. More than 100 years ago, Walt Whitman expressed this great central fact of America: "Here is not merely a nation, but a teeming Nation of nations."

Although the ingenuity and acts of courage of these immigrants, our ancestors, shaped the North American way of life, we sometimes take their contributions for granted. This fine series, *The Peoples of North America*, examines the experiences and contributions of different immigrant groups and how these contributions determined the future of the United States and Canada.

Immigrants did not abandon their ethnic traditions when they reached the shores of North America. Each ethnic group had its own customs and traditions, and each brought different experiences, accomplishments, skills, values, styles of dress, and tastes in food that lingered long after its arrival. Yet this profusion of differences created a singularity, or bond, among the immigrants.

The United States and Canada are unusual in this respect. Whereas religious and ethnic differences have sparked intolerance throughout the rest of the world—from the 17th-century religious wars to the 19th-century nationalist movements in Europe to the near extermination of the Jewish people under Nazi Germany— North Americans have struggled to learn how to respect each other's differences and live in harmony.

Our two countries are hardly the only two in which different groups must learn to live together. There is no nation of significant size anywhere in the world which would not be classified as multi-ethnic. But only in North America are there so *many* different groups, most of them living cheek by jowl with one another.

This is not easy. Look around the world. And it has not always been easy for us. Witness the exclusion of Chinese immigrants, and for practical purposes Japanese also, in the late 19th century. But by the late 20th century, Chinese and Japanese Americans were the most successful of all the groups recorded by the census. We have had prejudice aplenty, but it has been resisted and recurrently overcome.

The remarkable ability of Americans to live together as one people was seriously threatened by the issue of slavery. Thousands of settlers from the British Isles had arrived in the colonies as indentured servants, agreeing to work for a specified number of years on farms or as apprentices in return for passage to America and room and board. When the first Africans arrived in the then-British colonies during the 17th century, some colonists thought that they too should be treated as indentured servants. Eventually, the question of whether the Africans should be treated as indentured, like the English, or as slaves who could be owned for life was considered in a Maryland court. The court's calamitous decree held that blacks were slaves bound to a lifelong servitude, and so also were their children. America went through a time of moral examination and civil war before it finally freed African slaves and their descendants. The principle that all people are created equal had faced its greatest challenge and survived.

Yet the court ruling that set blacks apart from other races fanned flames of discrimination that burned long after slavery was abolished—and that still flicker today. Indeed, it was about the time of the American Civil War that European theories of evolution were turned to the service of ranking different peoples by their presumed distance from our apelike ancestors.

When the Irish flooded American cities to escape the famine in Ireland, the cartoonists caricatured the typical "Paddy" (a common term for Irish immigrants) as an apelike creature with jutting jaw and sloping forehead.

By the 20th century, racism and ethnic prejudice had given rise to virulent theories of a Northern European master race. When Adolf Hitler came to power in Germany in 1933, he popularized the notion of an Aryan race. Only a man of the deepest ignorance and evil could have done this. *Aryan* is a Sanskrit word, which is to say the ancient script of what we now think of as India. It means "noble" and was adopted by linguists—notably by a fine German scholar, Max Müller—to denote the Indo-European family of languages. Müller was horrified that anyone could think of it in terms of race, especially a race of blond-haired, blue-eyed Teutons. But the Nazis embraced the notion of a master race. Anyone with darker and heavier features was considered inferior. Buttressed by these theories, the German Nazi state from 1933 to 1945 set out to destroy European Jews, along with Poles, Gypsies, Russians, and other groups considered inferior. It nearly succeeded. Millions of these people were murdered.

The tragedies brought on by ethnic and racial intolerance throughout the world demonstrate the importance of North America's efforts to create a society free of prejudice and inequality.

A relatively recent example of the New World's desire to resolve ethnic friction nonviolently is the solution that the Canadians found to a conflict between two ethnic groups. A long-standing dispute as to whether Canadian culture was properly English or French resurfaced in the mid-1960s, dividing the peoples of the French-speaking Province of Quebec from those of the English-speaking provinces. Relations grew tense, then bitter, then violent. The Royal Commission on Bilingualism and Biculturalism was established to study the growing crisis and to propose measures to ease the tensions. As a result of the commission's recommendations, all official documents and statements from the national government's capital at Ottawa are now issued in both French and English, and bilingual education is encouraged.

The year 1980 marked a coming of age for the United States's ethnic heritage. For the first time, the U.S. Bureau of the Census asked people about their ethnic background. Americans chose from more than 100 groups, including French Basque, Spanish Basque, French Canadian, African-American, Peruvian, Armenian, Chinese, and Japanese. The ethnic group with the largest response was English (49.6 million). More than 100 million Americans claimed ancestors from the British Isles, which includes England, Ireland, Wales, and Scotland. There were almost as many Germans (49.2 million) as English. The Irish-American population (40.2 million) was third, but the next-largest ethnic group, the African-Americans, was a distant fourth (21 million). There was a sizable group of French ancestry (13 million) as well as of Italian (12 million). Poles, Dutch, Swedes, Norwegians, and Russians followed. These groups, and other smaller ones, represent the wondrous profusion of ethnic influences in North America.

Canada too has learned more about the diversity of its population. Studies conducted during the French/English conflict showed that Canadians were descended from Ukrainians, Germans, Italians, Chinese, Japanese, native Indians, and Inuit, among others. Canada found it had no ethnic majority, although nearly half of its immigrant population had come from the British Isles. Canada, like the United States, is a land of immigrants for whom mutual tolerance is a matter of reason as well as principle. But note how difficult this can be in practice, even for persons of manifest goodwill.

The people of North America are the descendants of one of the greatest migrations in history. And that migration is not over.

Koreans, Vietnamese, Nicaraguans, Cubans, and many others are heading for the shores of North America in large numbers. This mix of cultures shapes every aspect of our lives. To understand ourselves, we must know something about our diverse ethnic ancestry. Nothing so defines the North American nations as the motto on the Great Seal of the United States: *E Pluribus Unum*—Out of Many, One.

Three serious-faced Amish boys watch a farm sale near Strasburg, Pa. This particular auction raised money for the local fire company.

Preface:

THE PLAIN PEOPLE

Within a few hours' drive from the heavily populated cities of the northeastern United States is an area of Pennsylvania where a group of people preserve a way of life entirely different from that of modern America. In southeastern Pennsylvania, primarily in the beautiful rural area of Lancaster and Berks counties, live the Amish people, who practice the customs and beliefs that have been passed down to them for almost 300 years.

CLOTHING

Present-day sightseers who see the Amish for the first time often feel as if they have stepped back into another century. The Amish regulate every facet of their existence according to their literal interpretation of the Bible. These people, who speak a dis-

Schoolboys peek out from under their straw hats on a sunny day. As Amish children grow up they often care for their younger siblings, helping them learn responsibility and persuading them to be obedient.

tinctive German dialect known as "Pennsylvania Dutch," wear clothing and maintain an unusual hairstyle prescribed by custom. The women and girls part their hair in the middle, and both sides are pulled tight around the back and rolled into a bun. They never cut their hair or curl it. Men and boys let their hair cover their ears and have long sideburns. Married men have beards, but single men are clean-shaven. Moustaches are forbidden.

Amish men wear black or dark blue jackets without lapels and loosely fitting pants held up by suspenders. No zippers, belts, or buttons are used; their clothing is held closed by hooks and eyes—a holdover from an earlier time in Europe when buttons were unknown. Neither jackets nor pants have pockets. Shirts are usually white, and no ties are worn. An Amish man is seldom seen without a hat— a broad-brimmed black felt hat or, in warm weather, a straw hat with a black band.

Amish women dress alike, wearing long, full-skirted dresses that nearly reach the ground. All the dresses are the same style, as if they were made from the same pattern. An apron is worn over the dress, with unmarried women wearing a white apron and married women either a black or darkly colored one. Only solid, somber colors are permitted—no plaids, stripes, checks, or bright colors are worn. This severely plain dress is devoid of any frill that might indicate worldly vanity. Amish women wear a white cap on the back of their heads with a bow under the chin. In colder weather the women wear heavy crocheted shawls, and the men use long black overcoats. Children are dressed in the same style as the adults. Almost all the clothing is made at home by the women. No one wears jewelry. The Amish have kept the same style of dress for centuries. Any divergence from the old styles is regarded with suspicion.

Who are these people who avoid the 20th century, who refuse to use electricity in their homes, own automobiles, radios, or television sets and do not go to the movies? Who are these people who adhere to a simple agricultural life, tilling the soil with horse-drawn plows, and who harvest their crops with sickles and scythes, leading an anachronistic lifestyle as they steadfastly reject the comforts and pleasures of modern technology?

POPULATION

The Amish were among the first people to seek religious freedom in the American colonies. In the early part of the 18th century, Amish immigrants fled religious persecution in Germany and Switzerland to settle in Pennsylvania, where they purchased tracts of rich farmland and established their own self-sufficient communities. While Amish communities died out in Europe by 1900, they have prospered in North America.

Although the Old Order Amish in Lancaster, Pennsylvania, receive the most attention from the

An Amish couple take their two small children out for a ride in their horse and buggy. Differences in carriage structure, decoration, and harness vary from one Amish community to another and are subject to the rules (*Ordnung*) of each order.

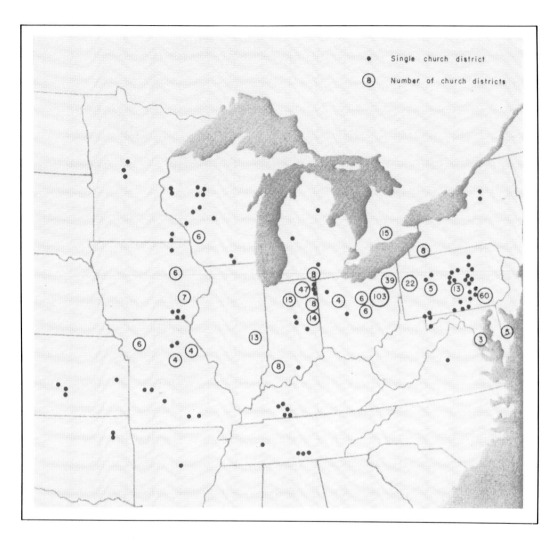

A map depicting the different Amish settlements in North America.

outside world, Amish communities as a whole are more numerous and diverse than is popularly thought. There are Amish settlements in 20 states—the vast majority in Pennsylvania, Ohio, and Indiana—as well as in Ontario, Canada. These communities differ in the conservatism of their beliefs and practices, with some groups rigidly upholding tradition and others adapting more to the modern world. The entire Amish population, though, is distinguished by its dramatic lack of assimilation into

American society. With their distinct community, the Amish are living proof that an ethnic group can resist the American "melting pot" and preserve its own religion, language, and culture.

The Amish have remained highly insulated from the outside world. Few "English," as they call outsiders, have joined the community because the Amish do not believe in seeking new members or engaging in missionary work. Nearly all the Amish are direct descendants of the first settlers. (In Lancaster County, five family names are held by more than 70 percent of the Amish population.) In fact, almost all Amish are distantly related to each other because endogamy is practiced—an Amish person must choose a mate from within the sect.

Despite the lack of new converts and the temptations to assimilate into society, the number of Amish continues to steadily rise. All birth control methods are prohibited and infant mortality is relatively low, so the birthrate is quite high. The average married couple has six or seven children, and it is not unusual to find families of ten or more. On average, more than 80 percent of the children choose to be baptized into the Amish faith as adults, a remarkably low dropout rate.

The Amish community has grown exponentially. An example of this is one Amish man who had 410 living descendants at the time of his death at age 95: 5 children, 61 grandchildren, 338 great-grandchildren, and 6 great-great-grandchildren. Altogether, the group's numbers have risen from less than 1,000 in 1800 to nearly 5,000 in 1900 and to more than 125,000 today. In Holmes County, Ohio, alone there are roughly 35,000 Amish, and the Lancaster group is 16,000 members strong. This unique community is comparable to one huge extended family. It is this family structure that effectively perpetuates Amish culture, faith, and traditions.

A tourist bus speeds past an Amish buggy on a street in Lancaster County. The Lancaster County Amish were once the most trusted group among their peers in matters of religious orthodoxy. They are now regarded as lax by some western Amish communities for allowing even limited farm mechanization.

TOURISM

Ironically, the simple, unpretentious Amish way of life has spawned a major multimillion-dollar tourist industry. In fact, the Amish and their towns—with such strange names as Intercourse, Bird in Hand, Ronks, Fertility, Bareville, Goodville, Blue Ball, and Paradise—rank among the top tourist attractions of the United States. Each year more than 3 million people travel through Lancaster County to view the Amish going about their daily tasks in an idyllic pastoral setting, with well-kept farms, one-room schools, and horse-drawn buggies. Unlike reconstructed villages such as Williamsburg, Virginia, and Sturbridge, Massachusetts, where costumed actors play a role, the Amish are a genuine rustic community.

An island of calm in a rapidly changing, highly technological world, the Amish community has grown increasingly fascinating to the rest of American society. Amish culture was featured on Broadway in the 1950s in the musical comedy *Plain and Fancy*. The popular 1985 movie *Witness,* starring Harrison Ford and Kelly McGillis, combined elements of romance and suspense in a story of the modern world's intrusion into one Amish family's life. Although often portrayed as quaint and peculiar, the Amish way of life appeals to many Americans seeking a return to old-fashioned values and a simpler, less hectic way of life.

Unfortunately, this fascination has contributed to rampant commercialization in Lancaster County, with dozens of gift shops, motels, and tour buses clogging the roads in Amish territory. Despite being regarded by so many as museum pieces, the Amish remain reserved and polite to tourists. Perhaps it is their strong faith that sustains them, their belief that God has called them to a life of hard work and humility. Without this dedication, the Amish might have disappeared many decades ago.

An Amish girl waits at the family buggy for her parents to return. Girls between the ages of four and six learn housekeeping and cooking skills while boys the same age begin to learn the basics of farming.

HISTORY
OF
THE AMISH

For the 300 years of its existence, Amish culture has perpetuated the customs and religious beliefs of its founders with scarcely any variation. To comprehend their resistance to change, it is necessary to understand Amish religious history. This firmness of religious belief is carried over into every aspect of Amish culture. In fact, tradition is the cornerstone of their fellowship.

PROTESTANT REFORMATION

Amish history has its roots in the complex and far-reaching European Protestant Reformation of the 16th and 17th centuries. The Protestant Reformation, or Protestant Revolt, like the Renaissance, was a general reaction against medieval civilization. Although primarily a religious movement, the Protestant Ref-

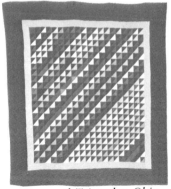

Diagonal Triangles, Ohio

Chapter openings show the brilliant varieties of textile folk art in these quilt patterns.

A depiction of the St. Bartholo-mew's Day Massacre (1572), a slaughter of Protestants by Catholics that began in Paris on August 24 and spread throughout France. Within weeks 10,000 Huguenots had been killed. The Protestant leader, Admiral Coligny, was decapitated (right, center) and his head sent to Rome.

ormation profoundly affected the social, intellectual, and political life of Europe. Spiritually, the new Protestant religions challenged the Roman Catholic Church's claim to being the only religion through which individuals could achieve salvation. From the worldly point of view, the Reformation involved a struggle between the power of the all-embracing medieval Church and the rising national states. It was, in effect, a rebellion against the religious, political, and economic control wielded by the Catholic Church.

Martin Luther (1483–1546) was the leading figure in the opening phase of the Reformation. Originally, his purpose was to reform what he considered to be evils within the Catholic Church. Many in the Church, however, opposed Luther. Basically, Luther questioned certain practices within Catholicism that had become a standard part of the religion but, according to his reading of the Bible, were not practiced at the time of Christ. Several powerful German princes, who opposed the papal claims of universal authority, zealously supported Luther for their own political reasons. It was this support that gave the Reformation its impact and brought about the collapse of papal authority in a large part of Germany.

Above: Martin Luther posts his 95 Theses on the church door in Wittenberg, Germany. One practice he condemned was the Catholic policy of indulgence, which gave papal absolution for a sin in exchange for an act of penance. Penance could include participation in the Crusades; usually it was a financial contribution to the Church. Luther believed that penance could only be offered to God.

Left: Portrait of Martin Luther by the great Northern Renaissance artist Hans Holbein the Younger. Luther decided to become a monk after he was struck by lightning and survived. Later he became disenchanted with aspects of Roman Catholicism and led the Protestant Reformation.

THE SWISS REVOLT

A 16th-century portrait of Huldreich Zwingli, the great Reformation leader, who preached that anyone, even non-Christians, could enter heaven if they led decent lives. The Swiss leader's liberal views prompted Martin Luther to label him a heretic. Zwingli was killed during later Catholic-Protestant violence.

Independent of Luther, a similar reform movement started in Switzerland at almost the same time. Led by Huldreich Zwingli (1484–1531), the movement also aimed to correct alleged abuses within the Catholic Church. Zwingli derived much support for his own convictions from reading Luther's early pamphlets. Although he denied being a disciple of the German leader, many of Zwingli's ideas markedly resembled those of Luther.

From his pulpit in Zurich, Zwingli demanded immediate religious reform. In 1523, the Zurich city council held a series of debates. As the basis for his arguments, Zwingli prepared 67 statements, or theses, which contained the essence of his ideas. In them, he asserted the sole and absolute authority of the Bible and affirmed the doctrine of salvation by faith—that is, one can hope to have an eternal life based on faith alone.

Zwingli rejected many of the most fundamental tenets of Catholicism. He rejected the papacy, saints, fasts, pilgrimages, monastic orders, the priesthood, holy relics, indulgences, the sacraments of Mass, confession, and absolution, and the concept of purgatory. Many of his proposed reforms were even more extreme, more austere, than those of Luther.

Soon, under Zwingli's influence, the city of Zurich abolished the Mass. Religious statues, pictures, crucifixes, altars, and candles were removed from the churches. Relics were destroyed. Holy water was done away with, and even church frescoes were covered with whitewash. To Zwingli, since none of these practices could be found in the Bible, they were evil and detracted from the true spirit of Christian belief.

Zwingli's reforms were more thorough than those of Luther, but both men agreed on the basic doctrines of Protestantism. On one main point, however, they had a fundamental difference—on how to interpret the Last, or Lord's, Supper, the meal Jesus and his disciples had on the eve of his crucifixion. Belief in this event is fundamental to all Christians. Luther held that in the Eucharist (a rite commemorating Christ's sacrifice), "This is my body" must not be interpreted literally. His is the theory of *consubstantiation* (where the wafer and wine of the Eucharist do not become the body and blood of Christ, although after consecration, Christ's flesh and blood co-exist in the bread and wine) as contrasted with the Catholic belief in *transubstantiation*, where the bread and wine are considered to be literally transformed into the flesh and blood of Christ. Zwingli, on the other hand, regarded the bread and wine of the Eucharist only as symbols of the body and blood of Christ. In 1529 Luther and Zwingli engaged in a series of debates in Marburg, Germany, but their differences on the Eucharist proved irreconcilable. Luther refused to change his interpretation, which to Zwingli was but another relic of Catholicism. This profound disagreement on the fundamental Christian ceremony marked the first major division in Protestantism—and led to the creation of two new churches—Lutheran and Reformed.

Conflicts between Catholics and Protestants caused much of Europe to seethe in religious and political turmoil throughout most of the 16th and 17th centuries. And, almost from the beginning, there were dozens of splits among the Reformed (Zwingli) group. In 1525, also in Zurich, Konrad Grebel (c. 1498–1526) became the leader of a small group who questioned some of Zwingli's reforms, especially his emphasis on the baptism of infants, as opposed to baptizing adults who could declare their beliefs. Should the religious fellowship initiate in-

An Amish bookplate in an 1814 copy of the Mennonite prayer book, *The Martyr's Mirror*. This bookplate, executed in 1896, was decorated with Fraktur, a form of calligraphy used in Amish books since the late 1700s.

fants or mature believers? Should the fellowship be expansive or limited? Over this major issue of baptism, the Grebel followers, who came to be known as Anabaptists (a name given them by their opponents), broke with Zwingli. The true church, according to the Anabaptists, was to be composed of a voluntary group of disciplined adults and would not attempt to embrace the whole of humanity.

The Anabaptists, who would be severely persecuted for their beliefs, refused to baptize their children as ordered by the Zurich city council. They could not find a scriptural justification to support infant baptism. They would not accept any governmental authority over religious practices. Many historians credit the Anabaptists with being the first religious movement to preach total separation of church and state. This group, which separated from the Zwingli-controlled church, became known as the Swiss Brethren, or Mennonites, after Menno Simons (1496–1561), a Catholic priest who joined the Brethren in the early days and became one of its most influential leaders.

Zwingli led the persecutions against the Brethren, forcing them to flee Zurich. To the Brethren, or Mennonites, Luther and Zwingli were partial reformers. They sought to complete the work of these two men by attempting to interpret the Bible literally, without interference from any governmental authority. Their goal was to return to Christianity as it was practiced in the time of Christ. Because they accepted literally the Sermon on the Mount as the example for Christian behavior, the Brethren would not fight for or take an oath upholding any civil government. These ideas caused them to be branded as heretics by civil and ecclesiastical authorities.

The Mennonite book, *The Martyr's Mirror*, recounts the cruel tortures inflicted by both church and state on these early followers. To practice their religion as they understood it and to escape persecution, many Mennonites migrated to the New World, especially to Pennsylvania, a haven of religious freedom.

THE MENNONITE-AMISH SPLIT

The Mennonites, like so many other religious sects, experienced dissension over religious doctrine. In 1693, a Swiss Mennonite elder, who felt that his religion had lost its purity, broke with his church and formed a new religious sect. His name was Jakob Ammann (c. 1644–1730), and his followers are called Amish. The Mennonites and Amish, therefore, have common religious and historical roots.

Mennonites in 17th-century Europe. The family depicted in this drawing seems serene, showing no trace of the hardships that impelled them to emigrate to America.

Perhaps the most important reason that the followers of Jakob Ammann separated from the Mennonites (1693–97) had to do with the practice of *meidung*, or the shunning, of excommunicated members. As Mennonites spread through Europe, differences developed over what to do with an adherent who violated the teachings of the religion and the sanctity of the fellowship. In some areas, wayward members were shunned at the communion table; in other areas, the errant ones were totally shunned not only in religious observances but in social and economic matters as well.

Jakob Ammann, who lived in the Swiss canton of Bern, believed that the general prevailing policy of shunning was not severe enough—that expelling a member from the communion was too lenient a punishment for those who had deviated from the religious fellowship. Ammann insisted that shunning must be total. He even demanded that the wife and children of an excommunicated member be prohibited from eating at the same table with the sinner, and that sexual relations should not occur between husband and wife until proper penitence had been made and restoration to the church obtained. He based this on the Biblical passage (1 Corinthians 5:11): "But now I have written unto you not to keep company, if any man that is called a brother be a fornicator, or covetous, or an idolator, or a railer, or a drunkard, or an extortioner, with such a one do not eat." Ammann also favored uniformity in dress and hairstyle. This aggressive leader began holding communion services twice instead of once each year, and he introduced the practice of footwashing, a reenactment of the biblical account of Jesus washing the disciples' feet (John 13), a rite also observed twice a year.

The followers of Ammann, who equated strictness with divine sanction, and those who did not

A farmer's market in Lancaster, Pa., provides farmers with the opportunity to sell directly to consumers. Such markets, common in Amish communities, help supplement family income.

An Amish man drives past a red schoolhouse in Lancaster County. Amish children still study from *McGuffey's Reader*, originally published in 1835.

At this livestock auction in New Holland, Pa., Amish and non-Amish intermingle. The straw hats of the Amish, are handmade. The hatmakers dry the straw, braid it, sew it together, and then shape the headgear.

"Rent a farm, milk cows, learn a trade, if possible, do manual labor as did Paul, and all that which you then fall short of will doubtlessly be given and provided you by pious brethren."
The words of Menno Simons, written in the 16th century, hold true for the Amish today.

accept his literal Biblical injunctions as the basis for every aspect of life, could not resolve their differences. Ammann's supporters split with the Mennonites to form a new religious sect—the Amish. It is estimated that of the 69 Swiss and German ministers involved in this theological debate concerning the purity of the religion, 27 sided with Ammann. Reconciliation efforts failed, and a new sectarian movement began.

Although much of the bitterness between the Mennonites and the Amish has subsided and these two Anabaptist groups have lived as neighbors for almost 300 years, the divisions still persist despite their common religious and historical roots. The main issue dividing them has almost always concerned lifestyle rather than basic Christian doctrine. In general, the Amish tend to be more conservative. They avoid modern technology. Most Amish, for example, use horse-drawn carriages, dress plainly, do not use electricity, and stress occupations involving the farm and home. Emphasis is placed on the local fellowship group. The Amish also forbid higher education for their members. Mennonites, on the other hand, are more accepting of education and 20th-century science and technology. Mennonites also support worldwide missionary activities as a way of enlarging the fellowship. The fundamental issue, now and in the past, has been the purity of religious practice.

IMMIGRATION TO THE NEW WORLD

The first Amish faced tumultuous conditions in Europe, with state and religious authorities waging a vicious campaign to extinguish the Anabaptist movement. Thousands were imprisoned, tortured, and even burned at the stake for their religious beliefs. Already wary of outsiders, the Amish sought refuge in isolated, mountainous farming areas throughout Switzerland, France, Germany, Holland, and Russia. Although some European nobles who valued the renowned Amish agricultural skills encouraged the group to settle in their territory, land shortages prevented most Amish from forming their own self-sufficient communities. This lack of opportunity, coupled with continuing religious persecution, spurred many to immigrate to the New World. Those Amish who stayed behind were unable to preserve their unique culture and merged with the Mennonites, completely losing their Amish identity by the end of the 19th century.

Religious dissenters who left Europe for America discovered unheard of freedom in Pennsylvania. William Penn, who had been jailed and harassed in England for his Quaker beliefs, founded Pennsylvania with a specific pledge of religious liberty for all. The state became a sanctuary for numerous religious groups—including the Amish, Mennonites, German Baptist Brethren (Dunkers), Moravians, Catholics, and Jews—who had encountered intolerance elsewhere. The first permanent Mennonite settlement in the New World was established in Germantown, Pennsylvania, in 1683. By 1727 the Amish began to emigrate from Switzerland and elsewhere in Europe. They found an abundance of arable land where they could farm successfully and practice their faith freely. Many of the Pennsylvania communities they developed in the 1700s have survived largely unchanged.

ARRIVAL IN CANADA

For several Amish families, even Pennsylvania of the 18th century was too strife-ridden. The American

This portrait of William Penn, who founded Pennsylvania in 1682, was painted about 1666. Around that time Penn's conversion to Quakerism, begun when he was at Oxford, became complete. His father beat him for his Quaker beliefs. Penn was sentenced to the Tower of London after he wrote *The Sandy Foundation*, a strong attack on Anglicanism.

Revolution reminded them of the wars in Europe and of the persecution that their ancestors had endured because of their pacifist views. Even though the Continental Congress granted the Amish community exemption from military service during the American Revolution, several families began the trek on foot or by Conestoga wagon to the remote territory then known as Upper Canada. After having lost all their possessions en route, the first Amish group arrived at the Niagara River in 1776. At that time Canada did not have a central government with sufficient authority to issue land grants, so the newly arrived Amish became squatters in the territory. They chose to settle on land covered with black walnut trees because these trees grow in limestone soil, the kind best suited for farming. Thus, Essex and Kent counties in southeastern Ontario have had Amish settlers since 1778.

Around 1796, the governor general of Canada advertised the availability of Canadian land in Pennsylvania newspapers, and another small group of Amish emigrants made their way to Ontario. They brought healthy cattle, sturdy furniture, and funds to buy good land. During the 1800s, more waves of Amish from both America and Europe arrived in the area. The Amish settlement in Ontario, which has not been as exposed to the inroads of tourism and modernization, continues to prosper today and retains some ties to the larger Amish community in the United States.

EXPANSION AND DIVISION

Although the Amish accept change slowly and reluctantly, their community has not remained stagnant over the years. As the Pennsylvania settlements prospered and grew, they had to make certain adjustments. While some Amish moved to Canada, many more spread out to the rest of the country. Pennsylvania farmland became scarcer and more expensive due to the rapid growth of families and the ongoing influx of new immigrants. Always searching for more affordable and more remote land, groups of Amish began settling in Ohio in 1807; they were among the first settlers in the Iowa Territory in the early 1840s. Gradually Amish communities sprung up in states as far-flung as Maryland, Oklahoma, and Michigan. As late as the 1960s, some Amish moved to British Honduras (now Belize) and Paraguay to establish new settlements.

Besides the scarcity of land, divisions within the community have also motivated Amish migrations. Major differences of opinion usually revolve around the meidung and how strictly to enforce shunning. In 1910, for instance, a rift developed in the Pennsylvania Amish community because a minister would not shun his son for becoming a Mennonite. Groups discontented with the community's decision on such matters would often splinter off and move to a place where they could start their own settlement.

The issue of modernization has also sparked much debate since America began growing less rural and more technologically advanced. As more contentions arose, the Amish Ministers' Conference stopped meeting in 1879, and distinctions between the "Old Order" Amish and those who moved closer to the Mennonites began to appear. The Amish were

A sleigh is used during winter to take children to and from school. Amish children once attended public schools, but have recently built their own one-room schoolhouses such as this one.

An Amish family drives a mule-drawn wagon loaded with all their household possessions. An airplane in the background provides a sharp contrast in transportation between the Amish and their neighbors.

at first permissive about much of the new farm technology that came into use in the early 1900s, but many feared drifting too far toward modernism; some technology was banned altogether, while other elements were adapted to fit traditional Amish beliefs. For instance, steel-wheeled tractors may be used around the barn to provide enough power to blow silage to the top of tall silos, but horses and manual labor are used in the field.

When compromise is not possible, further divisions occur. In 1927, the Beachy Amish, named for the bishop who led them, split with the Old Order to form a branch that is less strict about shunning and more permissive about the use of technology such as electricity, the automobile, and the telephone. After Old Order ministers met in the 1960s to evaluate the new farming equipment that had come into use and ended up banning almost all the modern harvesting equipment, the New Order Amish left the fold as well. Thus the Amish community continues to meet change in a variety of ways while still adhering to the core of their religious beliefs.

THE AMISH AS AMERICAN CITIZENS

No matter how much they adjust to modern technology, the Amish uphold a firm social separation from

Below: Late summer signals the time for the wheat harvest to these Amish farmers. Pennsylvania has been renowned for the quality of its wheat since the 18th century.

In 1957, this Amish man registered to serve jury duty on a murder trial where the accused allegedly killed an Amish farmer in Ohio. The juror faced a moral conflict because the prosecutor asked for the death penalty, but Amish belief does not hold with capital punishment.

the rest of American society. Besides their unique style of dress and dialect, they have their own businesses, community organizations, and often their own schools. While buying from and selling products to the outside world, the Amish socialize only with other Amish and Mennonites and spurn any cultural interaction.

However, the Amish are U.S. citizens and do contribute to the larger society. They serve on juries and pay all taxes except Social Security, whose bene-

fits they refuse. While never seeking public office, many Amish register to vote and cast their ballots in local elections important to them. Some Amish men join their local volunteer fire department, while others agree to help science by participating as subjects in genetic research. Their religion forbids them from fighting, but they have proven their loyalty during wartime by doing alternate service with civilian groups. Although remaining outside the modern world, the Amish willingly accept their social responsibilities.

Young children peep out the rear of their buggy. Parents encourage their sons and daughters to express their emotions freely, but do not allow sulking or self-pity.

PRACTICES
AND
BELIEFS

Religion is central to Amish culture. For these people, life has no purpose apart from service to God. The Amish adhere to a Christian faith in which the Scriptures dictate every aspect of life. Thus, the Bible is not only a religious text, but a strict guide to everyday living as well.

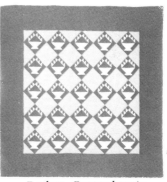

Baskets, Pennsylvania

The Amish do not believe in formal church buildings. They meet in various homes for Sunday services, which are held every other week. The place of meeting is rotated, usually on an annual basis. Church membership consists of adults who have voluntarily committed themselves to the fellowship and to the discipline of their fellow believers. Amish settlements are divided into districts, and each district consists of about 75 baptized members. If the district becomes much larger, it is again divided. Visiting the services of other districts is encouraged, and the great intermingling of the Amish diminishes any formal barriers among districts.

Buggies lining an Amish farm lane on a Sunday morning in Lancaster County indicate that an Old Order Amish worship service is about to begin. The Amish "meetings" take place in the homes of members. Note the traffic signs on the buggies.

In the religious hierarchy, there are bishops, ministers, and deacons. The bishop, the chief religious figure, can serve several districts. He performs marriages, baptisms, admits new members, and supervises the moral behavior of his flock. If there is any disciplinary action to be taken against a member, it is the bishop who determines the punishment. The ministers conduct the Sunday services and deliver sermons. The deacons handle administrative and financial matters affecting the district, and also assist poor members. Donations are accepted twice a year, and there are no collections at a service.

No formal training or apprenticeship is required for church officials. No special ceremony of ordination takes place. On the contrary, ministers and deacons are chosen from the men of the district by drawing lots. When an office is to be filled, can-

Joan. 18. † Der Han wirdt nit kråyen, biß du
d   mich drey mal hast verlöugnet.

Das XIV. Cap.

Ein schöne predig in deren er seine jünger ver=
manet zů leyden und gedult, zů demüt,
glauben, und liebe. Er verheißt auch inen
den geyst.

A   Nd er sprach zů seinen
jüngern: Euwer hertz
erschräcke nitt. Glau=
bend ir in Gott, so
glaubend auch in mich.
In meines vatters
hauß sind vil wonungen. Wo aber das
nit wäre, so hette ich es euch gesagt:
Ich gon hin euch wonung zebereyten.
Und ob ich hin gang euch die statt ze=
bereyten, wil ich doch wider kommen.
und euch zů mir nemmen, auff das
Joan. 8. b   ir sygind wo ich bin. † Und wo ich
hin gon, das wüssend ir, und den
wäg wüssend ir auch.

Spricht zů im Thomas: Herr,
wir wüssend nit wo du hin gaast, und
wie mögend wir den wäg wüssen?
Jesus spricht zů im: Ich bin der wäg
Joan. 1. a   und die warheyt und das † läben.
11. c   * Niemants kumpt zum vatter dann
* Joan. 6. c   durch mich. Wenn ir mich kanntind,
so kanntind ir auch meinen vatter.
Und von nun an kennend ir jn, und
habend jn gesehen. Spricht zů im
Philippus: Herr, zeig uns den vat=
ter, so benügt uns. Jesus spricht zů
im: So lang bin ich by euch, und du
hast mich nit erkennt? Philippe, wär
mich gesehen hat, der hat den vatter
gesehen. Und wie sprichst du dann,
Joan. 10.   Zeig uns den vatter? † Glaubst du
c   nit das ich im vatter, und der vatter
* Joan. 3. c   in mir ist? * Die wort die ich zů euch
7. b 8. c   red die red ich nit von mir selbs: der
12. f 14. c   vatter aber der in mir wonet, der
selb thůt die werck. Glaubend mir
das ich im vatter, und der vatter in
mir ist: wo nit, so glaubend mir doch
B   umb der wercken willen. Warlich
warlich ich sag euch: Wär in mich
glaubt der wirt die werck auch thůn die
ich thůn, und wirdt grössere dann dise
Matt. 21. c   thůn: dann ich gon zum vatter. † Und
Mar. 11. c   so ir etwas werdend den vatter in mei=
Joan. 15.   nem Nammen bitten, das wil ich
a 16. c   thůn, auff das der vatter gepreyset
werde in dem sun. So ir etwas bit=
tend in meinem Nammen, das wil
ich thůn.

Liebend ir mich, so haltend meine
gebott. Und ich wil den vatter bit=
ten, und er sol euch einen anderen trö=
ster geben, das er bey euch bleybe
ewigklich [namlich] den geyst der
warheyt, welchen die welt nit mag
empfahen, dann sy sicht jn nit, und
kennet jn nit: ir aber kennend jn,
dann er bleybt by euch, und wirdt in
euch sein. † Ich wil euch nit weysen   Psal. 45. a
lassen, ich komme zů euch. Es ist   Matt. 28. c
noch umb ein kleine zeyt so wirdt mich
die welt nit mer sehen, † ir aber söl=   Joan. 20.
lend mich sehen: dann ich läb, und ir   b c d 11. a b
söllend auch läben. An dem selbigen tag
werdend ir erkennen das ich im vatter
bin, und ir in mir, und ich in euch. † Wär   Joan. 15.
meine gebott hat, und haltet sy, der ist's   a
der mich liebet: wär mich aber liebet,   1. Joan. 5.
der wirdt von meinem vatter geliebet   a
werden: und ich wird jn lieben, und
mich selbs jm offenbaren. Spricht zů
jm † Judas, nit der Iscariotes: Herr,   Acto. 15. c
was ist's dann, das du uns wilt dich
offenbaren, und nit der welt? Jesus
antwortet, und sprach zů jm: Wär   C
mich liebet, der wirt mein wort hal=
ten, und min vatter wirt jn lieben:
und wir werdend zů jm kommen, und
wonung bey jm machen. Wär aber
mich nit liebet, der haltet min wort
nit. † Und das wort das ir hörend,   Joan. 3. e
ist nit mein, sonder des vatters der   7. b 8. c 12. f
mich gesendt hat.   14. a

Sölichs hab ich euch gesagt, die=
weyl ich bey euch gwesen bin. Aber
der tröster der heilig geist, † welchen   Acto. 2. a
mein vatter senden wirt in meinem   2. Tim. 1. a
Nammen, * der selbig wirt euch alles   * Joan. 16.
leeren, und euch erinneren alles deß   b
das ich euch gesagt hab.

Den friden laß ich euch, meinen
friden gib ich euch: nit gib ich üch wie
die welt gibt. Euwer hertz erschräcke
nit, und förchte sich nit. Ir habend
gehört das ich euch gesagt hab: Ich
gon hin, und kumm wider zů euch.
Hettend ir mich lieb, so wurdend ir
euch fröuwen das ich gesagt hab, Ich
gon zum vatter: dann der vatter ist
grösser dann ich. † Und nun hab   Joan. 13.
ich's euch gesagt, ee dann es geschicht,   b 16. a
uff das wenn es nun geschehen wirt,
das ir glaubind. Ich wird hinfür nit
vil mit euch reden, Dann es kumpt
der † fürst diser welt und hat nichts   Joan. 12.
an mir. Aber uff das die welt erken=   b

p   ne

A page from the 1744 edition of a 16th-century Swiss New Testament printed in Fraktur, a heavy, black-letter typeface favored by early German printers and still used by the Amish.

didates are suggested by other church officers and by members of the district. At a Sunday service, those nominated are called to the front of the room, where there are as many Bibles as candidates. Each is instructed to turn to a given text. The one who finds a slip of paper at that page is the new official. The bishop is chosen by lot from among the ministers. Each district has a bishop, two ministers, and a deacon. The Amish believe that selecting church officials by lot enables God to choose the best man. Women are not permitted to serve in leadership positions within the church; although limited to the domestic realm, the central importance of home and family assures women great respect within Amish society.

SUNDAY MEETINGS

According to tradition, men and women are separated at these Sunday services. If there is not enough space in one room, the single members are placed in other rooms, where they are also separated by sex. When the service begins at about 8:30 AM, with all seated on wooden benches, the men remove their hats. Hymn singing opens the service, but musical instruments are forbidden. The tunes have been passed down for generations, as the hymn books have only the words.

The Amish use the *Ausbund* hymnal, which consists of about 50 hymns. It is the oldest Protestant hymnal in use in America. The first edition was printed in 1564 by Anabaptists in Germany. Although Mennonites no longer use these hymns, they are still sung by the Amish. Basically, they are tales of the suffering, humiliation, and torture endured by the ancestors of the Amish. The hymns describe the sorrow of a people who tried to protest against the wickedness of this world and tell of those who

attempted to crush their righteousness. Instead of being melancholy, the hymns speak of conviction, of courage, and of the assurance that God will not forsake his own but will lead them through sorrow to an everlasting life. There is no particular order in which the hymns are sung. An elder will call out a hymn, set the pitch, and the congregation will follow. The "Hymn of Praise" is the one most often sung. Other, more sprightly, hymns are reserved for special occasions, such as weddings.

After the singing a sermon in High German follows, lasting about 30 minutes. The minister who is to preach is chosen by other ministers present on the day of the service. Sermons are extemporaneous. It is believed that in this way the word of the Lord will come through. Silent devotion follows. Next, the deacon reads from the Bible, followed by another minister's longer sermon, also in High Ger-

Amish *Ausbunds* (hymnals) printed in 1767 and 1801. Many of the lyrics of Old Order Amish hymns are quite gruesome, most having been written by 16th-century martyrs awaiting their death sentence. The music is based on Gregorian chants, folk tunes, and other melodies.

man. (The Amish use a Bible printed from old metal plates, which they own and lend to a local printer.) Subsequently, the congregation hears personal testimonials. The service ends with a benediction. An average Sunday service lasts about three hours. There is little variety in format. Emphasis is on the past — past suffering, past hardships, and past martyrs.

Following Sunday church services, a meal is served. The bishop, ministers, and deacons eat first, followed, in order, by older married men, younger married men, women, and, finally, the children. Men and women eat separately. When one is finished eating, the dishes are passed to the next without washing them but merely wiped clean with a piece of bread. The meal is practically standardized to avoid competition among the host families— bread, jellies, pickles, cheese, coffee, and fruit pies

The Amish children perform Christmas carols for their mothers in a one-room school near Kalona, Iowa. Married women wear traditional white hats, or *Kapps* and unmarried women wear black hats for services, white hats at home.

are served. Everyone is expected to remain for this meal, which is also a grand social occasion. The rest of Sunday is reserved for visiting relatives.

RITES AND CEREMONIES

Communion is one of the most important parts of Amish religious activity. It is held twice a year, in the spring and the fall. The communion service is considered a demonstration of the unity of the religious community and shows that no major rifts or divisions exist among the membership. Approximately two weeks prior to the ceremony, a one-day service of self-examination is held. All church members are usually present. The bishops and ministers state the church rules. Each member is then asked if he or she agrees with the rules and is at peace with the other members. The service itself is simple, but it is the most revered of all the ceremonies. The preachers pass pieces of homemade bread and a large cup filled with wine to each communicant. In High German, the words "This do in remembrance of Me . . ." are intoned.

Following communion, the ceremony of foot-washing occurs. The members are divided by sex. The men and women then form pairs and wash each other's feet. This ritual is followed by the exchange of the "holy kiss" between the pair (2 Corinthians 13:12). The footwashing reflects the humility of the members and also symbolizes the washing and purification of the soul in the blood of Christ (John 13:4–17).

Baptism, when new members are initiated into the fellowship, is held before the second of the semiannual communion services in the fall. Like other Anabaptists, the Amish view baptism as an act that demands a total personal commitment, so they refuse to baptize infants. New members are generally over 16.

Young people are given an opportunity to change their minds because it is better to not take the vow than to do so and later break it. Consequently, teenagers are allowed to sow some wild oats—going to movies, drinking, driving, and even owning cars—and face the temptations of the outside world before they commit to the Amish faith. In her book *Plain and Simple,* Sue Bender explains, "Worried parents looked the other way and hoped that with patience the seeds of family loyalty and group harmony they had planted would grow."

Having been prepared for this special day for years by their families and communities, roughly four out of five young adults decide to join the church. They take instruction in Bible study and church rules, and a few months later the bishop baptizes them by pouring water over their heads. Once a young person is baptized, he or she is a full church member responsible for obeying the *Ordnung,* or the rules of the church. If a baptized person violates these strictures or chooses to abandon the faith, he or she will be shunned. Because of this intense commitment, the percentage of those baptized who eventually leave the church is extremely small.

While the Amish do not recognize national holidays, they do observe some religious holidays. On these days, no unnecessary work is done. The Amish fast on Good Friday and before the spring and fall communions. Easter, Ascension Day, Pentecost, Thanksgiving, Christmas, New Year's Day, and Epiphany are other special days. In keeping with the austere traditions of the Amish, at Christmas there are no trees, colored lights, or Santa Claus, but the children do receive gifts. The Amish also make holidays out of joyous celebrations such as marriages.

Amish buggies are a common sight on many of the country roads of Lancaster County. Because of their religious beliefs, Old Order Amish residents of the area depend on the horse and buggy rather than cars for transportation.

MARRIAGE

When a couple wants to marry, the prospective bridegroom notifies the deacon, who confidentially inquires if the bride's parents approve. Rarely, if ever, does an Amish marriage occur without parental approval. If nothing stands in the way, the bishop announces the planned marriage about two Sundays before the formal vows. Engagements are not festive or romantic. Young couples meet at church services and holiday songfests. All relatives and friends are invited to the wedding, which is an elaborate social affair.

The marriage service itself takes place either on a Tuesday or a Thursday, traditionally in November after the harvest. The bishop presides. Gowns and tuxedos are forbidden. There are no kisses, rings, photographers, florists, or caterers. The groom wears his Sunday clothing, and the bride, for the first and only time in her life, wears a white garment. After the simple ceremony, a day of feasting and singing follows. The bride and groom spend their wedding night at the bride's home. There is no honeymoon. In fact, the couple do not live together until the following spring after a rather ritualistic period of weekend visits with family and friends.

Parents assume responsibility for the new couple's farm. Family and friends provide furniture, quilts, rolls of linoleum, home-canned foods, farm tools, and the other basic necessities needed by the newlyweds. The new couple always receives a great deal of support from parents and friends. Marriages last a lifetime because divorce is unthinkable in Amish society. Desertion and separation are practically unknown. The Amish frequently remarry after the death of a spouse. Out of respect for the deceased, however, the widow or widower does not usually remarry until at least a year has passed. The ceremony for a second wedding is even more simple than for the first.

"DUST TO DUST..."

The Amish maintain simple burial and funeral rites. Some Amish communities embalm the bodies but most do not. The deceased is prepared for burial by family and friends. The tasks of informing relatives, preparing the burial site, and constructing the plain pine coffin, are carried out by relatives and neighbors. The immediate family is relieved of all farming and domestic responsibilities as others take over these tasks. No payment of any kind would ever be considered for this assistance.

The funeral is usually held three days after the death. Amish funerals are large affairs, with relatives and friends often coming from long distances to attend. There is a sermon but no eulogy. Instead, the bishop or ministers stress the fact that the Bible admonishes everyone to be ready for death. The young are reminded that death is inevitable and that one should live so as to be prepared for it. Every Amish community has a small cemetery; usually a corner of a field is fenced off for that purpose. There are no family plots. The concrete headstones on the tombs record only the name of the deceased and the dates of birth and death. The Amish regard life as a means to "store up treasures in heaven," and death is looked upon as a natural part of the life cycle, when one's reward is realized.

A young Amish boy with his
father during a sale of household goods and antiques in
Ohio. Amish parents are lov-
ing but firm with their children.

THE HOME
AND
THE FARM

The Amish countryside of Lancaster County forms one of the most picturesque rural scenes in America. The bucolic setting, with its charming country lanes and roads, is pastoral life at its best. A sense of peacefulness and tranquillity prevails over the area.

The spacious farmhouse is the center of Amish life. There, babies are born and church services are held, as are weddings and funerals. The windows have shades but no curtains or blinds. No pictures or mirrors hang on the walls. There are no musical instruments of any kind. But colored, braided rugs, pillows, quilts, and spreads are everywhere. Hand-wound wooden gingerbread clocks are on the mantels. The simple furniture and chests are often decorated with old Pennsylvania Dutch designs. An indescribable beauty and charm permeate the stark simplicity.

Log Cabin, Barn Raising design, Ohio

All furniture is handmade. Boys learn carpentry at an early age and assist in making and repairing household articles. Amish women make most of the clothing for the families, as well as the lovely quilts. Although there are numerous "Amish quilts" offered for sale in the Lancaster area, few are authentic as the genuine ones are considered family heirlooms and are passed down. The farms and handmade furniture are also handed down from generation to generation and are seldom sold.

Many Amish homes, which have no electricity or telephones, are comprised of several houses that have been built onto the original structure. In these separate but attached sections parents live in one building and grandparents in another. Thus, two or three generations generally live under the same roof. In contrast to industrial societies where care of the elderly has become a major problem, the Amish extended family system eliminates the need for nursing homes for the elderly. Older people do not retire but rather withdraw gradually from farm work, at which time the younger family members take over the farm chores and move into the main house.

The three-generation house is a distinctive characteristic of the Amish. One of the dwelling units is the "grandfather" house, where the older couple moves when they retire, leaving the main responsibility of house and farm to the younger couple. Also pictured is a windmill, which the Amish use instead of electric power to draw water.

The Amish faithfully support each other and rarely accept outside help, such as medicare, from the government. Because the elderly are cared for by their own, Congress, in a special ruling, exempted self-employed Amish from paying the Social Security tax. The Amish do not refuse modern medical treatments and go to local hospitals when necessary, but home remedies are stressed. Good food, tea and vinegar, and homemade herb preparations are the standard medicines. Above all, it is family and friends who nurture and care for the sick and the elderly. Mutual aid, from birth to death, is at the center of Amish health care.

CUISINE

The large kitchen is the center of activity and the most important part of the house. Amish men read the Bible there, children play games, and the women cook. Lighting is by kerosene or gasoline lamps. A wood- or coal-burning stove is used for cooking and heating, although many Amish kitchens now have more modern gas ranges. Often there is no plumbing, and water must be brought in from outside for cooking, drinking, and bathing. Traditionally, perishable food was kept in a springhouse, but many Amish now have gas-powered refrigerators or rent freezer space at local markets. While it is common to find vinyl flooring and gas-powered equipment in newer Amish kitchens, the taboo against electrical appliances remains.

The cuisine prepared in these kitchens is hearty and traditional, using the meat, dairy, and produce from the family farm. Some typical dishes are: sausages of every type, bacon, sauerkraut, chicken-corn soup, chow-chow (spicy relishes), bread, apple butter, and jellies of every description. Nearly every meal ends with a fruit pie or a shoo-fly pie. In addi-

WET BOTTOM PENNSYLVANIA DUTCH SHOO-FLY PIE

Syrup Filling:
1 cup molasses—dark
1 cup hot water 1 level tsp. soda
*   dissolved in the boiling water*
3 eggs
Stir and let cool

Crumb Topping:
4 cups flour
1 cup brown sugar
½ tsp. mixed spices: salt, nutmeg, ginger,
*   cloves, cinnamon, mace*
½ cup shortening (no butter)
Combine ingredients to form crumb
*   mixture for pie topping.*

Have two 9-inch unbaked pie shells ready. Pour syrup filling in crusts, dividing portions equally. Sprinkle crumb topping over syrup mixture, dividing topping equally between the two shells. Leave a little "air" in the center of the pies to allow for expansion and to prevent mixture from "boiling over." Bake 1 hour to 1 hour-10 minutes in 350 to 375 degree oven.

A recipe for one of the most traditional Amish dishes, shoo-fly pie. Tourists often go to farmer's markets in Lancaster County to buy this special treat.

tion to canning vegetables and preserving fruit, many households make their own cider, root beer, and ginger ale. This homey food is popular at local markets and restaurants.

SOCIAL LIFE

Visiting is the most important social activity for the Amish, adding to the strong family and community cohesion and solidarity. A major social event for the young unmarried Amish are "singings," which are held almost every Sunday evening, often at the same place the church services were held. Church hymns are sung and refreshments are served. Local public sales or auctions provide occasions for more social activity. Few Amish in the area will miss an auction, which often takes on the atmosphere of a small fair, with men and women gathering in separate groups, talking and chatting.

RELIGION AND THE LAND

"To every thing there is a season, and a time to every purpose under the heaven: a time to be born, and a time to die; a time to plant, and a time to pluck up that which is planted. . ." (Ecclesiastes). Following Biblical injunctions, the Amish feel it is their responsibility to till the soil and bring forth an abundant harvest. They believe that farmers live especially close to God and nature, and they cherish both the hard work and the peacefulness of their rural environment. The Amish strive to remain close to the land, minimize contact with outsiders, and avoid cities, which they view as sinful and corrupt like Sodom and Gomorrah. Consequently, most Amish cultivate the soil or work in craft-related trades such as harnessmaking, blacksmithing, and carpentry.

Unfortunately, as land has grown scarcer and costlier, farms have become smaller and more specialized. As many as one-third to one-half of Amish men must now pursue work outside the farm. In the 1970s and 1980s, many cottage industries, such as machine shops and crafts stores, sprung up in the Amish community. Some men labor part-time on construction crews, while women may teach before marriage and later bake or cook for local restaurants. However, working the land remains central to the Amish.

Amish boys dressed up for Sunday service. During the time between adolescence and marriage, teenagers must decide whether they want to become baptized and join the Amish church.

Their religious convictions strongly influence their farming methods. The Amish farm, which averages about 80 to 100 acres, is an old-fashioned family farm, with labor done by men, women, and children. Traditional methods are upheld, while field tractors and mechanical milking machines are spurned. If technology does not conflict with their religion, however, it may be adopted by more permissive Amish sects. For instance, Amish may use air-powered tools or harness the energy from batteries

or tractor engines to do work around the barn. In addition, Amish mechanics adapt modern machinery, such as the hay baler, so that it can be pulled by horses. Dairy farmers especially have had to modify their equipment to meet milk company standards. While accepting a measure of modern progress, the Amish remain committed to avoiding industrialization, using horses, keeping their farms on a small scale, and providing valued work for the whole family.

A hitch of six mules is being led along a country road by an Amish farmer. The Amish use draft animals for farm work, and mules are popular with some farmers because of their endurance and the fact that they eat less than horses.

In Lancaster County, Pennsylvania, an Amish family uses a mechanical tobacco transplanter in a field. While the farmer guides the mules that pull the machine, the girl in front places the tobacco plants between two revolving disks. The two boys follow the transplanter and mark missed plants with pegs.

Right: Water wheels provide power for Amish family farms. The sign points to the springhouse, a farm building adjoining a pond or spring and often used for food storage or as a dairy. Crocks and cans are placed in the stream so that they are kept cool.

Though lacking time-saving technology, Amish farms are highly productive. Crops include corn, hay, potatoes, beans, and fruit. Tobacco is a chief cash crop (tobacco use in pipes and cigars is traditional among the Amish, although cigarettes are frowned upon and smoking is discouraged altogether in some groups). Most farms also produce beef, pork, and poultry, and much of the acreage is devoted to raising feed for the livestock. The Amish at work in these fields with their teams of horses is a scene out of the past and a living testimonial to their religion.

Many of the Amish views of farming find resonances in the environmental movement. Implicit in Amish culture is the view that people are the caretakers of God's earth, not exploiters of it. The beauty

Amish farmers harvest corn. Because the Amish try to be self-sufficient, they prefer to raise a diversity of crops. However, the steadily diminishing size of their farms has forced them to become more specialized and to raise cash crops.

Right: An Amish man drives a wagon loaded with corn. In the 18th century, the Amish depended on wheat as a main source of income, but 200 years later corn is the more profitable crop.

In Lancaster County an Amish farmer reaps a bountiful wheat harvest. About one-fourth of the county's farmland is owned by the Amish, who continue to employ agricultural methods that predate the Industrial Revolution.

Four young Amish boys bring in a load of tobacco from the fields. Tobacco requires more hand labor than many other crops, but the Amish have the patience and the manpower to grow it successfully. Tobacco is an extremely profitable crop in Lancaster County.

Amish farmers load corn fodder into a horse-drawn baler. After the corn is harvested, the stalks are shredded sometime in November and used as livestock feed.

in the universe is perceived in the orderliness of the seasons, the intricate world of growing plants, the diversity of animals, and the forces of living and dying. People must work in harmony with nature, the soil, and the weather. Farming in a way that causes the soil to lose its fertility is considered sinful and is a charge that can even be brought before the church members, for they believe in the Biblical injunction that "he who robs the soil of its fertility sins against God and man." They must leave the soil to the next generation in as good a condition as when they inherited it. In keeping with this belief, few Amish farmers would think of using synthetic fertilizers, insecticides, or pesticides. Using organic fertilizer such as manure is considered a superior farming practice because it is a more natural one.

That Lancaster County ranks first in farm income in the United States is due largely to the hard work of the Amish. The rolling pastures where sheep and cattle graze, the fields of tall golden grain, and the long rows of tobacco provide a patchwork of magnificent colors. Every season has farm scenes unequaled in their simple beauty, a reminder of the pre-industrial age when human and animal labor provided the basic necessities of life. And yet, the Amish are able to grow and raise enough food for their families, store adequate provisions until the next harvest, and still have surplus to sell at markets.

Left: An Amish man drives his horses past a neighboring farmer's tractor. Despite their rejection of mechanized farm machinery, the Amish often have their fields plowed and planted before those of conventional farmers.

Below: Riding down a country lane, these Amish pass a bountiful harvest scene in Lancaster County. One reason for such a concentration of Amish in Lancaster County was the Amish preference for its limestone soils, which they believed superior to any other type.

COMMUNITY AND ASSISTANCE

Springing from a western European background, the Amish believe in the private ownership of property; the family is at the core of Amish life and the home is the center of worship, so each married man should have his own family farm. However, their practice of mutual assistance results in what could be called a semicommunal society. Christian brotherhood is an important tenet of their faith. Although every Amish farmer operates as a separate economic unit, each can always rely on his fellow church members,

The Sugar Creek Budget.

Vol. 1.　　　　　　SUGAR CREEK, O., MAY 15, 1890.　　　　　No. 1.

J. C. Miller,　　　　　Proprietor.
J. M. Richardson,　　　　Editor.

TERMS:

50 cts. a year in advance.

THE BUDGET.

In presenting to the public the first issue of the Budget we feel that sense of humility that usually emanates from a knowledge of the criticisms which our little paper and all others of its kind usually meet on being introduced to the reading public.

But dear readers all we ask is that we may meet your recognition

It is not our object to attempt social, political, or religious reforms

It would seem that a new publication brought out without any of these objects was without purpose. Such however is not the case.

Our purpose is to conduct our newspaper in the interest of our village and the vicinity, to give the current news, and to aid in propagating any movement for the general good.

We do not look for our support to sectional jealousies, or contentions between different villages or localities, but desire the patronage of all and distribute all favors equally.

Independent in all things, we maintain the ground of neutrality, and shall fearlessly publish whatever may be of interest and conducive of good morals.

A newspaper in a village, although a small one, is most surely beneficial, and every citizen interested in the prosperity, growth, or business affairs of his place should give it his support.

The Budget will be published regularly Semi-Monthly, and we hope that all who may read this copy have a kindly feeling toward this our first Journalistic enterprise, will make it manifest by sending in their subscriptions, and advertisements.

FINED.

Last Saturday night a young man living a few miles from Shanesville, visited that village, and filled up with tanglefoot.   On leaving town he saw fit to break off and destroy several ornamental trees, which Mr. J. H. Wallick had planted along the side walk in front of his residence. Mr. Wallick promptly got out a warrant and had him arrested and brought before Squire Zollars, where he plead guilty, and fine and costs were placed at about Nineteen Dollars.

This affair should teach some people that trees are not planted along the streets to be destroyed.

A great many people are in the habit of using ornamental and shade trees as hitching posts, and thus injuring and destroying them. The law is very strict in such cases. We withold the young man's name, hoping it will be a lesson for him, and that in the future he may not let Benzine and his baser propensities get the better of him

Mr. Moyer, father of our popular station agent, was in town last Tuesday and Wednesday, looking up the interests of the Canton Repository.

Several very fine large carp have been caught in Sugar Creek this spring. On last Sat. Mr. Levi Hostetler succeeded in landing one which measured 16 in. in length and weighed 2 3-4 lbs. and on the same day Mr. John Deetz captured one which weighed 3 lbs. Two yrs. ago several thousand young carp were placed in the creek by owners of ponds and the result speaks well for the deed.

If you desire to see a fine lot of ladies spring and summer hats call on Mrs. N. C. Beachy.   Mrs. B. evinces good taste in the artistic manner in which she trims them.

Miss Mary A. Miller has started a subscription school for primary scholars, and we learn she has secured quite a number of the little folks. Miss Miller is an energetic young woman and parents who have children of the school age should not neglect this chance, as it is much better to have them under the care of a kind and efficient teacher, than to have them running about the streets and sowing the seeds of vice.

Mr. E. Habenstein, of Mt. Hope gave us a look at his smiling countenance a few days ago. We learn he has been employed by N. C. Beachy as an agent for the Solid Comfort Plow.

The man who imagines he is a four horse team with a dog under the wagon sometimes has a bigger load than he can pull,

Get your Job Printing done at the Budget Office.

Page one of the first issue of the *Budget*, the Amish newspaper founded in 1890. This newspaper, which serves Amish and Mennonite communities, is published by a non-Amish press in Ohio.

not only for moral support but for financial help as well. If an Amish person needs money to purchase land, family members will loan it at about half the current interest rate charged by a commercial bank. With this ethic of self-help, the Amish discourage any investment from outside the community, and excess earnings are retained for loans to other Amish. Foreclosures are nonexistent, and bank failures or business bankruptcies do not affect them. If, on a rare occasion, it is necessary to borrow money from a bank, the loan is underwritten by the church district.

The Amish are aware of one another's needs because most families subscribe to a newspaper called *The Budget*. Published weekly in Sugar Creek, Ohio, by a non-Amish newspaperman, the paper carries news accounts from most Amish settlements throughout North and South America as well as of conservative Mennonite groups. Local contributors from each community provide accounts of births, marriages, deaths, accidents, and of any unusual happenings. Health matters, with weekly progress reports concerning the chronically ill, as well as farm sales, moves, and other local news appear in this newspaper. Occasionally, *The Budget* asks for financial assistance for an unfortunate Amish family, and it is not unusual for contributions to come from Amish communities throughout both continents.

All forms of government farm subsidies and disaster aid are refused. Since the Amish do not believe in commercial insurance on their property, local agreements call for community sharing of damages. If, for example, a member's barn is destroyed by fire, the community will rebuild it. Usually the farmer who suffers a loss due to fire or windstorm will pay one-fourth of the cost himself and the remaining three-fourths is divided among the community members. (Amish barns have no

An Amish farmer in Lancaster County transfers his tobacco harvest from the field to his shed where it will hang to cure. More than 10,000 acres of cigar tobacco are grown in the county, much of it by the Amish.

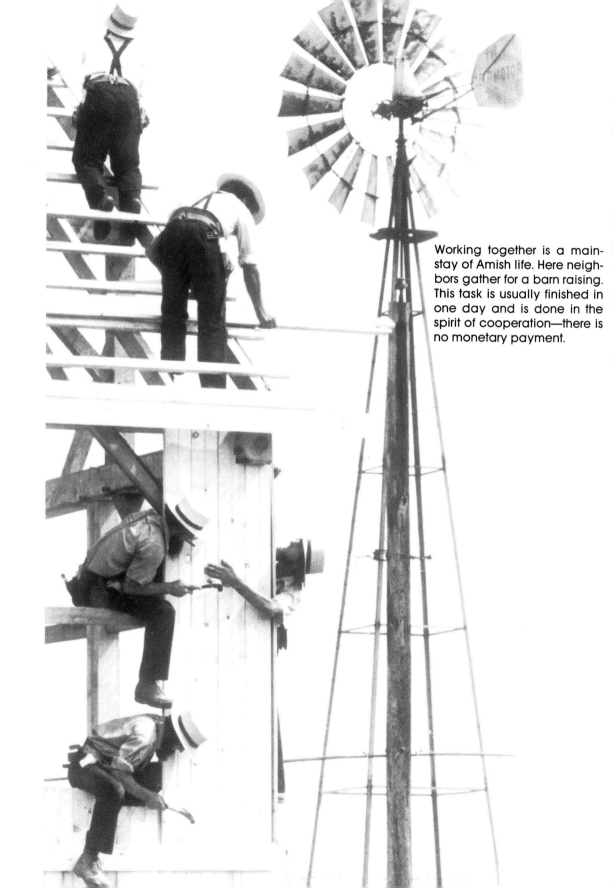

Working together is a main-stay of Amish life. Here neighbors gather for a barn raising. This task is usually finished in one day and is done in the spirit of cooperation—there is no monetary payment.

lightning rods because that, they believe, would be tampering with God's will.) About 200 Amish men can work all day "barn raising" without any financial return, and the women provide the noontime meal. Similarly, if a member is ill or incapacitated, the community will plow, seed, or harvest his fields. Faith and fellowship truly dominate every aspect of Amish life.

Scores of Amish farmers assemble to raise a new barn for another Amish family near Leola in Lancaster County. During the all-day barn raising, the women cook and provide meals and refreshments for the men.

Three children walk home from school on a scenic country road near Intercourse, Pa. The ungraded classrooms promote a sense of community among Amish schoolchildren, a quality that lasts throughout adulthood.

EDUCATION

One of the most crucial issues facing the Amish in the 20th century has been the preservation of their way of life against the inroads of modern civilization. This dilemma has been most acute in the area of education; here the right of the Amish to practice their religious beliefs undisturbed runs head-on against laws concerning compulsory education, a fundamental doctrine of democratic society.

Although the Bill of Rights does not guarantee free, compulsory education, it had been assumed since the founding of the United States that popular government requires a literate public. But it was not until the 1890s that most states adopted compulsory school attendance laws. Progressive educators, prompted by a desire to "Americanize" the large number of immigrants pouring into the country, pressed for more aggressive enforcement of edu-

Tree of Life, Ohio

cation laws. Several court cases upheld the concept of compulsory schooling on the grounds that it was essential for the "welfare of the minor" and that education safeguards the welfare of the community and the safety of the state.

The Amish are not against education but they are opposed to modern schools that teach more than the basic skills of reading, writing, and arithmetic. They see compulsory education as a force leading to assimilation with the outside world, and public schools are perceived as a serious threat to their homogeneity. The Amish oppose school busing and the use of audiovisual materials, as well as curriculums that include courses in career goals,

Father and son drive past a one-room school in Lancaster County. Although at home the Amish speak Pennsylvania Dutch, at school these children learn English.

athletics, music, the teaching of evolution, and the use of science laboratories. They also resist tenure for teachers, since God intended that the ill-prepared or poor teacher do some other kind of work. The Amish feel that education should prepare one for farm work or the ministry, and both vocations can best be learned from the family.

Thus, the Amish feel that not only is high school irrelevant for them but that by exposing their children to worldly values their chance of eternal salvation could be impaired. Greater learning might lead to pride and the temptation to pursue achievements in the outside world. In *Amish Society,* John Hostetler relates an Amish leader's representative view of education:

> We feel that anyone who is capable of making a decent living, helping his neighbors in need, raising a family that will be an asset to the community, and

Rows of old-fashioned desks await installation in an Amish schoolhouse in Lancaster County. One-room schools in the Old Order Amish parochial system provide students with a formal education through the eighth grade, after which children leave to help their parents full-time on the farm.

living at peace with God and his fellow men has attained about the most practical and best education there is to get. . . . What worth is an education if we do not have peace with God? What is education worth to us if we can't control our children?

To counteract this possibility, the Amish founded their first private school in 1925 in Delaware. A 1955 compromise by Pennsylvania governor George Leader allowed the Amish to set up their own vocational schools for children who had graduated from eighth grade but did not meet the minimum age for leaving school. However, conflicts over compulsory attendance laws and school science requirements continued to occur throughout the country. In some cases, Amish parents were fined or even jailed for their noncompliance with the laws. This deeply felt struggle over religious principle

After being sentenced to five days in jail for refusing to pay fines for not sending their children to high school, these Amish elders in Honey Brook, Pa., gathered to discuss strategy in 1960. They had refused to enroll their children because they considered the school "too worldly."

roused the sympathy of many non-Amish people and spurred the creation of the National Committee for Amish Religious Freedom in 1967. Continued Amish resistance set the stage for a dramatic court case involving the rights of a religious minority when in conflict with state education laws.

A classroom in a New Order Amish parochial school in Kinsman, Ohio. Compared to the Old Order, New Order Amish are considered more liberal in religious doctrine, even permitting some use of telephones, electricity, and tractors.

CONFLICT WITH SECULARISM

The case concerned the small Amish community of Green County, Wisconsin. The Amish first arrived in Green County in 1963. By 1968, there were 24 Amish families in the community. They had come searching for less expensive agricultural land. Sky-rocketing real estate values in Pennsylvania had made farming, particularly for young families, increasingly difficult.

From the time of their arrival, the Amish clashed with school authorities. One parent ob-

Barefoot Amish youngsters walk to their one-room school in Leacock, Pa. Amish schools have had trouble finding textbooks considered acceptable by the church elders. The Old Order Book Society prints many of the books used by Amish children.

jected, for example, to his daughter's attendance in a high school physical education class because she would be forced to wear shorts. Another opposed the teaching of evolution in the required science textbook. In 1968, public school authorities of Green County insisted that the small Amish community send their children to the local high school. The Amish refused, defying a Wisconsin state law requiring school attendance until the age of 16. The lower court upheld the school authorities. The case was eventually appealed to the Wisconsin Supreme Court, which ruled that enforced schooling of Amish children beyond the eighth grade was a violation of the free exercise of the religious rights of the Amish—a decision upheld by the Supreme Court of the United States.

In the landmark 1972 Supreme Court decision (*Wisconsin* v. *Yoder*), the Court voted unanimously to exempt the Amish from state compulsory attendance laws beyond the elementary grades. "It is neither fair nor correct to suggest that the Amish are opposed to education beyond the eighth-grade level," wrote Chief Justice Warren Burger. "What the record shows is that they are opposed to conventional formal education of the type provided by a certified high school because it comes at the child's crucial adolescent period of religious development." The Court ruled that the Amish did not pose a threat to public safety, but that forcing them to attend high school would violate their religious rights.

Today, Amish children attend local parochial one-room schoolhouses, which are ungraded. They do not attend high school. Amish families pay both the required local school taxes and support their own school system.

Although they recognize that formal education is useful, the Amish believe that the family is the

Laughing Amish schoolgirls enjoy recess in Leacock, Pa. As the number of Amish schools has increased, the Amish have provided teachers, usually single women, from their own community.

best teacher. At school, an Amish child can learn the three R's with his brothers, sisters, cousins, and friends, but the real education takes place in the home. Girls are taught to sew, cook, and bake. Boys learn carpentry and, above all, the skills of farming. These fundamentals cannot be learned in a schoolroom but must be learned by actual experience. Both boys and girls tend to farm chores, take care of animals, and help their parents in any way they can.

THE SCHOOL DAY

All Amish schools follow the same basic schedule, which is not much different from the traditional rural schoolhouses at the turn of the 20th century. The day is divided into four periods of approximately one-and-one-half hours each. There is a recess be-tween each period and a lunch break at noon. All schools begin the day with hymn singing in both English and German. Then there is a reading from the Bible. The children learn English (reading, grammar, spelling, penmanship, and composition) and arithmetic (addition, subtraction, multiplication, long division, percentages, ratios, and simple and compound interest). The techniques of New Math are not taught. Textbooks are quite old-fashioned by today's public-school standards. Some Amish schools use reprints of the original 19th-century *McGuffey Reader*, but even here, some of the stories are considered too patriotic and militaristic. Amish schools avoid fairy tales, myths, or stories in which animals talk, and anything dealing with sex. Every story must have a moral. Besides reading and writing in English, the children also study German so that

A group of young Amish men engage in a game of corner, or mush, ball, a favorite sport, as the girls watch. It is a rough sport. Players in each corner of a square try to hit their opponents in the center with a hide-covered ball of straw.

Laughing and jostling, these Amish boys enter their one-room schoolhouse after recess. With children of different ages and levels in one classroom, the teacher must spend part of each day concentrating on each age group.

they can understand the Amish Bible. Although religion is not taught in schools—the family and the church are considered the better teachers in that realm—Amish values such as humility and cooperation are reinforced in the parochial schools. When history is taught, the emphasis is on Amish history, but children learn the basic facts of American history, especially about the constitutional guarantees of religious freedom.

In essence the controversy between the Amish and secular officials over education—whether it be over curriculum, teacher training and certification, or state attendance laws—has to do with the simple fact that the American education system perpetuates certain social values that it feels represent the majority. The Amish, on the other hand, are concerned with maintaining their status as a minority and keeping their distinctive beliefs from being overwhelmed by the surrounding culture.

Despite modern styles, beach wear for the Amish shows how intent they are in retaining their deep-seated traditional way of life.

THE AMISH
TODAY

Bow Tie, Ohio

early 300 years ago, the Amish came to America like many other immigrant groups seeking religious freedom and affordable farmland. Unlike most other groups, though, the Amish have defied Americanization and maintained their distinct ethnic identity to a startling degree. Their anachronistic culture provides more than just a fascinating diversion for tourists—it offers important lessons about ethnicity, culture, and modern society in America and can serve as inspiration to other religious and cultural minorities. The Amish today illuminate many of the compromises, trade-offs, and challenges involved in actively preserving a unique community.

HEALTH

On the whole, the Amish tend to live longer than the general population. The number of deaths from cancer, heart disease, and circulatory, respiratory, and digestive ailments is much lower among the Amish than it is for the rest of the American population. The Amish lifestyle provides a model of good health in its comparative lack of stress and in the vigorous exercise of farmwork. In addition, the Amish eat organically grown food, with no preservatives or additives, and live in rural areas with little pollution and crime.

The Amish are not immune to health problems, though. The level of intermarriage in their society has resulted in a relatively high frequency of such genetic problems as anemia, phenylketonuria,

About one-half of the Amish population in the United States accepted vaccination against polio after the dreaded disease had crippled a number of Amish during an outbreak among them in 1979.

Joe King, an Amish man from Lancaster County, studies his portrait at a Lancaster art show. He is something of an exception among his peers since most Amish consider it vain to pose for paintings or photos.

hemophilia, dwarfism, deafness, and mental handicaps. Their infant mortality rate is also slightly higher than the national average, possibly as a result of infant deaths from birth defects.

Studies have shown that Amish communities suffer from many of the same problems as the outside society—alcoholism (some Amish even participate in Alcoholics Anonymous), juvenile delinquency, emotional problems, and suicide. Their suicide rate is as high or slightly higher than the national average; in *Amish Society,* John Hostetler notes that young men dealing with the stress of deciding whether to be baptized seem to be at particular risk. In recent years, the first two documented cases of murder within the Amish community have marred the usually serene society, but crime remains a rarity. Whenever possible, the Amish community attempts to handle these problems itself.

THE AMISH IN A MODERN WORLD

As the pace of technological advancement has accelerated in 20th-century America and more outsiders have encroached upon their once-isolated territory, the Amish have faced increasing pressures to assimilate. While steadfastly resisting great change, the Amish have wisely evaluated new technology and made concessions to modernism when possible. The compromises can seem endless and baffling to the outside observer: teenagers who wear running shoes under their traditional costume; farmers who

An Amish carriage being outfitted with blinking electric warning lights on its rear to comply with Pennsylvania state law. The carriage shop, owned by John Lapp, specializes in making the lights that are placed on the shafts of the vehicles.

use tractors in the barn but employ horses in the field to pull modern machinery; households that buy plastic dishes, vinyl flooring, handheld calculators, and other synthetic items; community members who will ride in cars but not drive them.

The choices can seem confusing, but Amish bishops carefully consider the ramifications of each adaptation. Their religion does not condemn electricity and technology but remains wary of their effects on society. For instance, there is nothing wrong with occasionally riding in a car, but owning one would lead to a drastic change in lifestyle. Besides being a vain status symbol, the automobile gives a mobility that would undermine small church districts and affect the slow pace of life.

The picturesque village of Intercourse, Pa., with Amish buggies lined up at a hitching post. Amish communities provide for themselves and others many services and tools made obsolete by modern American technology. Thus Amish insure their self-sufficiency in all their needs.

91

An Amish schoolgirl takes a swing during a softball game near Kinsman, Ohio. Amish families in this community built their own schoolhouse for their children.

Often changes are made for business purposes or for convenience as long as they do not fundamentally alter the Amish way of life. Amish women may use readily available polyester fabric but they still follow age-old patterns in crafting their clothes and quilts. Many Amish install telephones on street corners to conduct business or to use in case of emergencies, while keeping them out of their daily life. Amish farmers keep track of current advancements and adapt them to suit their old-fashioned, small-scale farms. Although some Amish men would see nothing wrong with using computers in their businesses, they have been banned because they are too close to television, a fundamental medium of the outside culture. In this continual balancing act, the Amish make some advantageous changes while scrupulously guarding their home life and their cultural distinctiveness.

Young Amish schoolchildren have to face the complex pressures of modern society while maintaining and continuing the Amish way of life.

Tension between the traditional and the modern continually develops and sometimes creates divisions from the Old Order Amish. On an individual level, some young adults choose not to be baptized. Estimates of the dropout rate range from 10 to 25 percent. Usually those who forgo baptism stay close to the Amish community and join a conservative Mennonite church.

Many factors account for this low dropout rate. The Amish community is small, tightly knit, and extremely supportive. Their life is relatively simple, unhurried, and stress-free, while the outside world appears unfamiliar and dangerous. Since Amish children attend parochial schools, they know few outsiders and are unprepared to compete in the modern world. The threat of being shunned also serves as a means of social control. Overall, the Amish community provides security, the comfort of a firm ethnic and religious identity, and an intense sense of belonging.

THE AMISH AND THE OUTSIDE WORLD

Despite their striking differences, the Amish and their "English" neighbors have always coexisted quite peacefully. Although local newspapers receive some letters to the editor grumbling about Amish parents allowing their children to work farm equipment or the effects horse-drawn buggies have on the roads, outsiders generally have a high opinion of the Amish. Their old-fashioned Christian values and strong work ethic are widely respected. When an arsonist torched several Amish barns in Belleville, Pennsylvania, in 1992, the misfortune received a great response. As Amish traveled from all over the state to help with the barn raisings, contributions poured in from English around the country. Local bank president William Hayes explained to *People* magazine, "The rest of us here feel—embarrassed is too light a word. It's important to us that the Amish know they're a valued part of our heritage."

In examining that heritage, many Americans are inspired to critique modern life and evaluate the "progress" that has been made. In March 1995, the *New York Times* reported on a growing movement based at the Center for Plain Living in Chesterhill, Ohio. The center and its magazine, *Plain,* encourage people to emulate the simpler lifestyle of the Amish, Mennonites, and conservative Quakers. The magazine already boasts several thousand subscribers and estimates that in the past year several hundred people in the Ohio area have adopted this plain way of life, rejecting technology and emphasizing the family. While few Americans are likely to relinquish their cars and televisions, many envy the Amish for their connection to the earth, the slower pace of their lives, and the strength of their families and communities.

It is a testament to the Amish people's faith that their distinct culture has not only remained alive but has thrived in America. Bucking the tide of dominant cultural messages, this unique ethnic group has retained a large degree of economic self-sufficiency, maintained control of their children's education, and limited contact with the government, the media, and other outside forces of change. In sacrificing a greater level of choice and individuality, they have gained a deeper group identity and sense of security. As new challenges arise, the Amish will likely continue to draw strength from their families, faith, and traditions, enabling them to endure.

FURTHER READING

Bender, Sue. *Plain and Simple: A Woman's Journey to the Amish*. New York: Harper & Row, 1989.

Fisher, Sara E. and Rachel K. Stahl. *The Amish School*. Intercourse, PA: Good Books, 1986.

Horst, Mel, and Smith, Elmer. *The Amish*. Whitmore, Pa.: Applied Arts, 1966.

Horst, Mel, and Smith, Elmer. *Among the Amish*. Allentown, Pa.: Pennsylvania German Folklore Society, 1959.

Hostetler, John. *Amish Life*. Scottsdale, Pa.: Herald Press, 1983.

Hostetler, John. *Amish Society*. Baltimore: Johns Hopkins University Press, 1963, 3rd ed. 1983.

Hostetler, John, and Huntington, Gertrude. *Children in Amish Society*. New York: Exposition Press, 1971.

Jordan, Mildred. *The Distelfink Country of the Pennsylvania Dutch*. New York: Crown Publishers, Inc., 1978

Kraybill, Donald B. *The Puzzles of Amish Life*. Intercourse, PA: Good Books, 1990.

Rice, Charles, and Steinmetz, Rollin. *The Amish Year*. New Brunswick: Rutgers University Press, 1956.

Schreiber, William I. *Our Amish Neighbors*. Chicago: University of Chicago Press, 1962.

Smith, C. Henry, *The Mennonite Immigration to Pennsylvania*. Norristown, Pa.: Pennsylvania German Society, 1929.

Smith, Elmer. *The Amish Today.* Norristown, Pa.:
    Pennsylvania German Society, 1961.
Warner, James, and Denlinger, Donald. *The
    Gentle People.* New York: Grossman
    Publications, 1969.
Wood, Ralph, ed. *The Pennsylvania Germans.*
    Princeton: Princeton University Press, 1942.

INDEX

PICTURE CREDITS

FRED L. ISRAEL is a professor of American History at the City College of New York. He is the co-editor of *A History of American Presidential Elections* and *The Justices of the United States Supreme Court*, also published by Chelsea House. His most recent work, in collaboration with Arthur M. Schlesinger, Jr., is *Running for President: The Candidates and Their Images*.

SANDRA STOTSKY is director of the Institute on Writing, Reading, and Civic Education at the Harvard Graduate School of Education as well as a research associate there. She is also editor of *Research in the Teaching of English,* a journal sponsored by the National Council of Teachers of English.

Dr. Stotsky holds a bachelor of arts degree with distinction from the University of Michigan and a doctorate in education from the Harvard Graduate School of Education. She has taught on the elementary and high school levels and at Northeastern University, Curry College, and Harvard. Her work in education has ranged from serving on academic advisory boards to developing elementary and secondary curricula as a consultant to the Polish Ministry of Education. She has written numerous scholarly articles, curricular materials, encyclopedia entries, and reviews and is the author or coauthor of three books on education.

ANNIE MCDONNELL has a bachelor of arts degree from Swarthmore College. She currently works as a book editor in New York City.

REED UEDA is associate professor of history at Tufts University. He graduated summa cum laude with a bachelor of arts degree from UCLA, received master of arts degrees from both the University of Chicago and Harvard University, and received a doctorate in history from Harvard.

Dr. Ueda was research editor of the *Harvard Encyclopedia of American Ethnic Groups* and has served on the board of editors for *American Quarterly, Harvard Educational Review, Journal of Interdisciplinary History,* and *University of Chicago School Review*. He is the author of several books on ethnic studies, including *Postwar Immigrant America: A Social History, Ethnic Groups in History Textbooks,* and *Immigration*.

DANIEL PATRICK MOYNIHAN is the senior United States senator from New York. He is also the only person in American history to serve in the cabinets or subcabinets of four successive presidents–Kennedy, Johnson, Nixon, and Ford. Formerly a professor of government at Harvard University, he has written and edited many books, including *Beyond the Melting Pot, Ethnicity: Theory and Experience* (both with Nathan Glazer), *Loyalties,* and *Family and Nation.*